Beautiful GALWAY

Connemara & The Burren

Featuring the photography of Michael Diggin, Bord Fáilte and Colour Library Books Ltd

Published in Ireland by Gill and Macmillan Ltd
Goldenbridge
Dublin 8

With associated companies in Auckland, Budapest, Gaborone, Harare, Hong Kong, Kampala, Kuala Lumpur, Lagos, London, Madras, Manzini, Melbourne, Mexico City, Nairobi, New York, Singapore, Sydney, Tokyo, Windhoek

Printed and bound in Singapore by Tien Wah Press
ISBN 0 7171 2070 8

Beautiful
GALWAY
Connemara & The Burren

Gill and Macmillan

Even those who know little of Ireland, its fascinations and attractions, have heard of Galway Bay. No doubt this is largely due to the famous song. And the sun going down on Galway Bay is, indeed, a remarkable sight.

The wide expanse of the waters, fringed to north and south by the rising hills of Connacht, reflect the red glare of the dying sun with eye-straining brilliance. But the waters of the Bay are not always kind. The rugged shores have claimed a daunting share of shipwrecks over the centuries, including the shattered remnants of the Spanish Armada.

Into the head of the Bay flows the Corrib River, and on its first crossing point stands Galway City. Traditionally rich from the wine trade with Spain, Galway has always been a maritime base; indeed, for many years the Mayor of Galway was automatically an admiral charged with patrolling the western approaches to Ireland, but that task ended last century. The magnificent mace and regalia of the mayor-admiral, however, remain, as does the rigid, 18th-century layout of central Galway. But it is not only the past which makes its presence felt forcefully in Galway City. A massive, domed cathedral completed in 1965 towers over the Corrib as testimony to the Catholic faith of the inhabitants.

For socialising it is difficult to beat Galway, particularly in August and September. In the former month, the Galway Races attract the superb horses of Ireland to compete for such prestigious trophies as the Galway Plate and the Galway Hurdle, both among the most highly prized by any trainer. September sees Galway immerse itself in the Oyster Festival. Founded on the legendary quality of the seafood from Galway Bay, the festival has gained worldwide renown. The climax of events is an oyster-opening contest in which chefs from around the world compete. Of rather more interest to the layman, however, are the huge quantities of shellfish on offer in the bars and restaurants of the city.

Reaching out around Galway Bay, west of Galway City, are the embracing arms of land which form Connemara, the wild and beautiful area which has enchanted visitors for generations.

On the southern shore of Galway Bay, in County Clare, lies the unique landscape of The Burren, a treasure house of historic ruins. Caherconnel is only the largest of several massive, stone ring forts which dominate the uplands of The Burren. Built around A.D. 750, by which time the political power of the region was on the wane, Caherconnell is one of the later ring forts. Other stone forts on The Burren speak of both the prosperity and warlike disposition of the former inhabitants, and tucked just below the highlands is Dunguaire Castle, a fine fortified house of a type which became popular among petty landowners during the turbulent 15th century.

However, the true glory of The Burren is not just its history, but its flora, which is unique. The limestone and shale that form the hills have given the soil a peculiar characteristic which only certain species can tolerate. Combined with this is an exceptionally mild and wet climate due to the Gulf Stream which sweeps just offshore. Orchids are among the most prolific wild flowers on The Burren, and the botanic interest is heightened by the presence of Mediterranean, alpine and arctic plants jostling each other for roothold among the rocks. Exactly how the seeds of maidenhair fern, blue gentian, birdsfoot trefoil, cranesbill and a host of saxifrages all came to lodge and grow in The Burren is a mystery, but however it came about the result is spectacular, especially in late spring when the bulk of species flower.

The limestone of The Burren has created another marvel, this time beneath the ground. Rainwater seeping through the porous rocks has carved out extensive cave systems, some accessible only to experienced potholers, but a few of which can be explored by the less expert. The most famous are the Aillwee Caves, where organised tours may visit the spectacular rock formations of the two-million-year-old caverns. Subterranean water of quite a different kind is to be found at Liscannor, where there is a spring sacred to St Brigid, which attracts many devout pilgrims.

North of Galway Bay spreads the majestic landscape of Connemara. Arguably the finest scenic area in Ireland, Connemara has achieved much-deserved fame. The beauty of the land is matched by the rural lifestyle of the population, both being a result of the poor and infertile soils which cover the uplands. Much of the best of Connemara is enclosed within Connemara National Park, which spreads around the conical summits of the Twelve Bens.

Most people come to Connemara to enjoy the scenery, and certainly the best way to do that is on foot. But the beauty of Connemara can be treacherous. Even in the midst of the hottest summer the mountain tracks are damp underfoot. Mist and rain can close down with little notice, making it easy to stray into the dangerous bogs of the area. Despite this risk, Connemara exerts its fascination, and the beauty is undeniable.

The turbulent waters of Galway Bay have for centuries been the focus of this area of Connacht. With the alluring attractions of The Burren, Connemara and Galway City added to the glory of the Bay itself, it is no wonder that Galway Bay has become immortalised in song. Nor any wonder that those who choose to explore the beauty behind the song find all their dreams fulfilled.

Left and overleaf: The mountain-locked inlet of Killary Harbour, one of the grandest pieces of coastal scenery in County Galway.

Top left and left: Coastal scenes around Tully Cross, County Galway. **Above and overleaf:** Killary Harbour near its head at Leenane. Some 40 feet beneath the water surface the bottom is almost flat, with secure holding ground, making Killary one of the best natural anchorages in Ireland.

These pages: The Gaeltacht of County Galway embodies for many people the rural face of old Ireland. Indeed, traditional rural scenes such as these can still be found in the more remote regions, but mechanisation is increasingly gaining a hold.

Right and overleaf: Kylemore Abbey, on the shores of Kylemore Lough, stands north of the Twelve Bens. The Abbey is the Victorian creation, based on Tudor designs, of Mitchell Henry, a rich northern English merchant. Henry drained extensive areas of lakeside bog for his famous gardens.

Above and right: The Connemara coast near Clifden, one of the larger towns in the area. **Top right:** Kingstown Bay, where the Galway coast pushes furthest out into the Atlantic Ocean.

Left: The market town of Clifden, in western Galway. In the early autumn, thousands flock here for the annual Connemara Pony Show, and the town remains popular year round as a convenient place from which to explore the Connemara countryside. A short distance away is the bog in which Alcock and Brown crashed after their historic, non-stop flight across the Atlantic Ocean in 1919.

Top left: The view west from Kingstown Bay. **Left:** Sunset at Clifden Bay. **Above:** A choppy sea off Slyne Head, arguably the westernmost island of Connemara. **Overleaf:** A tiny, whitewashed village on Kingstown Bay.

Right and overleaf: Scenery around the charming fishing village of Roundstone, the largest settlement for some miles in any direction. The region offers fine beaches and hill-walking, and is very popular with tourists.

galway

Above: A boat dragged ashore beside one of the many small lakes that lie scattered around Glinsk, near the Galway border with Roscommon. **Top right:** Bertraghboy Bay, near Roundstone. **Right:** Roundstone Harbour.

SAINT JUDE

Left: A tranquil sea at Carna, centre of the lucrative Galway lobster fishing industry, which sells its catch to the finest restaurants of Ireland and beyond. A festival of the local arts and traditional farming skills provides an attraction here for tourists in July.

Left: The peaks of Connemara National Park. **Above:** The Twelve Bens, the most dramatic mountains of western Galway, seen through the haze over Clifden Bay. **Overleaf:** Dawn on the Twelve Bens.

Left: The turbulent Owenriff River of County Galway, which runs down to the north shore of Galway Bay near Knock, a small village whose name drives from the Gaelic for 'the hill'. This is a tiny village tucked between the Knocknalee Hills and the sea, not the Knock of pilgrimage fame, which is situated in County Mayo.

Above: Ballynahinch Lake, which lies at the foot of the Twelve Bens. **Right:** A raging stream drops down from Bengower to Ballynahinch Lake. **Overleaf:** Derryclare Lake.

Left and overleaf: Lough Corrib, which measures 27 miles in length and is fringed to the north by numerous caves. **Above:** The Maumturk Mountains, which peak at over 2,100 feet and form a long ridge from Killary Harbour to Lough Corrib.

ÁRD RATHAIN
ARDRAHAN 5
T69
CINN MHARA
KINVARA ½
T69
LEADHBÁN
LABANE 6
5½
T69

Facing page and right: The remote island fortress of Dunguaire Castle, in Kinvarra Bay, which has been recently restored as a private residence.
Below: A scene in Kinvarra town, on the south shore of Galway Bay.
Overleaf: An aerial view of Kinvarra.

Above: Galway Cathedral, built during the 1960s and a rather controversial addition to the city. **Right:** Galway University, built in 1849 in the style of an Oxford College. **Overleaf:** The docks of Galway, an important port for six centuries.

Galway City has been a place apart almost from its founding by the Norman Burgos family in the 1220s. It has long monopolised trade in this region of Connacht and has become a centre for the arts and folklore. Many of the younger generation from Dublin and the east come here for summer breaks, adding to a youthful community based around the university and its lively social life.

PATRICK
CASEY
Pearse Square
Equal Status
Ragged
Teach Bawn
Ground Master
Slaney Corner
Hay Party
NOEL
PLATE
LUSKA
CARROW BOY
THE LADYS MASTERS
FETHARD FRIEND
CLASH OF THE ASH
DISTEMPER
FORTUNE SEEKER

JACKSON
MORIARTY
SYDNEY JACKSON

These pages: The Galway Races, which take place on the Ballybrit Racecourse, half-an-hour's brisk walk from the city. The races offer a strange mix of local country folk and Ireland's high society among the spectators.

Above: The Spanish Arch in Galway, where merchant ships carrying the profitable trade in Spanish wine berthed. **Top right:** Fishermen at Salmon's Leap weir. **Right:** Salthill, the popular seaside resort which adjoins Galway.

Left and below: The stone walls of Inisheer, the smallest of the Aran Islands. **Facing page:** The town of Kilronan, on Inishmore, is perhaps the most tourist-orientated part of the Arans. **Overleaf:** The stone fortress of Dun Eoghanachta on Inishmore, built some 500 years B.C.

These pages: Scenes on Inishmaan, the middle of the Aran Islands in size and position. Less frequented by tourists, Inishmaan preserves more of the unique cultural heritage of these islands on the edge of Europe.

Left: Bare limestone pavements on The Burren. The porous nature of the limestone and the chemicals which leach from it add their qualities to the stunning flora of the region.

Right: The Poulnabrone dolmen on The Burren of County Clare. These remnants of prehistoric burial grounds lie scattered over the region and argue for a sizeable population at the time of their construction.

These pages: The Burren landscapes are dominated by bare rock and open skies. Where plants can get a roothold, they tend to be a remarkable collection of alpine and arctic species found together nowhere else.

Above: The Burren. **Top right:** A thatched cottage near the town of Ballyvaughan, where many visitors stay to explore The Burren. **Right:** A canal lock at Lisdoonvarna, famous throughout Ireland as a spa town. **Overleaf:** The lake-dotted scenery of County Clare. **Last page:** The Poulnabrone dolmen.